THURGOOD
MARSHALL

CIVIL RIGHTS LAWYER AND SUPREME COURT JUSTICE

THURGOOD

MARSHALL

CIVIL RIGHTS LAWYER AND SUPREME COURT JUSTICE

by Brenda Haugen

Content Adviser: Gregg Ivers, Ph.D.,
Department of Government,
American University

Reading Adviser: Rosemary G. Palmer, Ph.D.,
Department of Literacy, College of Education,
Boise State University

Compass Point Books ✦ Minneapolis, Minnesota

Compass Point Books
3109 West 50th Street, #115
Minneapolis, MN 55410

Visit Compass Point Books on the Internet at *www.compasspointbooks.com*
or e-mail your request to *custserv@compasspointbooks.com*

Editor: Mari Bolte
Page Production: Blue Tricycle
Photo Researcher: Svetlana Zhurkin
Cartographer: XNR Productions, Inc.
Library Consultant: Kathleen Baxter

Art Director: Jaime Martens
Creative Director: Keith Griffin
Editorial Director: Carol Jones
Managing Editor: Catherine Neitge

Library of Congress Cataloging-in-Publication Data
Haugen, Brenda.
 Thurgood Marshall : civil rights lawyer and Supreme Court Justice / by
Brenda Haugen.
     p. cm. — (Signature lives)
  Includes bibliographical references and index.
  ISBN-13: 978-0-7565-1877-6 (library binding)
  ISBN-10: 0-7565-1877-6 (library binding)
  ISBN-13: 978-0-7565-2201-8 (paperback)
  ISBN-10: 0-7565-2201-3 (paperback)
1. Marshall, Thurgood, 1908-1993—Juvenile literature. 2. Judges—
United States—Biography—Juvenile literature. 3. African American
judges—Biography—Juvenile literature.
I. Title. II. Series.
  KF8745.M34H38 2007
  347.73'2634—dc22   2006027078
  [B]

MODERN AMERICA

Starting in the late 19th century, advancements in all areas of human activity transformed an old world into a new and modern place. Inventions prompted rapid shifts in lifestyle, and scientific discoveries began to alter the way humanity viewed itself. Beginning with World War I, warfare took place on a global scale, and ideas such as nationalism and communism showed that countries were taking a larger view of their place in the world. The combination of all these changes continues to produce what we know as the modern world.

Thurgood Marshall

Table of Contents

1 THE BIGGEST CASE OF HIS LIFE

In May 1954, attorney Thurgood Marshall was in Mobile, Alabama, for a speaking engagement. He planned to go next to Los Angeles, California. However, he received a phone call that changed his plans. He had to go to Washington, D.C. The U.S. Supreme Court justices had reached a decision in the case he had argued before them. Marshall caught the next flight to the nation's capital.

As Chief Justice Earl Warren read the Supreme Court's decision, Marshall could hardly contain his excitement. He realized he had just won the biggest case of his career—*Brown v. Board of Education*. The court unanimously struck down a legal principle referred to as "separate but equal." The justices ruled that public school segregation—separate buildings

Lawyers George E.C. Hayes, Thurgood Marshall (center) and James M. Nabrit congratulated each other following the Supreme Court decision that declared segregation in public schools unconstitutional.

Earl Warren was born March 19, 1891, in Los Angeles, California. After earning his law degree from the University of California at Berkeley, he served as attorney general of California for four years and as governor of the state for a decade. He ran as the Republican vice presidential candidate in 1948 with presidential candidate Thomas Dewey. The duo was defeated, however, by Harry Truman and his running mate, Alben Barkley. Warren would go on to serve as chief justice of the United States from 1953 to 1969.

for black students and white students—made black children feel inferior, or less important, and hampered their education. No longer would segregated public schools be lawful. Black students and white students could be educated the same way and not be forced to attend different facilities.

"I was so happy I was numb," Marshall said.

After answering reporters' questions, Marshall jubilantly lifted up a little white boy named Bill Greenhill. In joyous celebration, Marshall ran with the little boy on his shoulders through the marble halls of the U.S. Supreme Court building. What a sight these two made—a big black man and a little white boy bouncing through the halls of one of the country's most hallowed buildings. Bill's father, Joe Greenhill, knew Marshall. As assistant attorney general in Texas, Greenhill had once opposed Marshall in a court case. Now he was vacationing with his family in Washington, D.C. By chance, the Greenhills visited the Supreme Court on the day the decision

for *Brown v. Board of Education* was announced. Greenhill understood Marshall's excitement about the case and said:

After the Supreme Court ruling, schools began accepting both black and white students.

> *He picked up our son Bill and put him on*
> *his shoulders and ran down the corridor*
> *of the Supreme Court. He was having a*
> *good time, we were having a good time ...*
> *He just won a biggie.*

After returning little Bill to his family, Marshall quickly found a pay phone. He called the New York City office of the National Association for the Advancement of Colored People (NAACP), where he

The National Association for the Advancement of Colored People (NAACP) was established in 1909 by a group of 60 blacks and whites who were against the practice of lynching. They became committed to ending discrimination against blacks and other minority groups. Today the NAACP's membership numbers in the hundreds of thousands. With headquarters in Baltimore, Maryland, it remains active in fighting for equality for all.

worked as a lawyer. Though he had to shout to be heard over the noise in the crowded hallway, Marshall shared the good news with his staff before they heard it from someone else.

Despite his joy, Marshall knew the Supreme Court's ruling wouldn't end the battle against segregation. Many school officials, particularly in the South, vowed to fight integration of black students into all-white schools. Marshall predicted it would take about 10 years before all public schools in the United States were fully integrated. Many people found it hard to believe it would take that long. In reality, it would take much longer than anyone expected.

Marshall would spend most of his life fighting racism and working for equal rights for all Americans. As a lawyer for the NAACP, he would win many important landmark cases. Lawsuits such as *Brown v. Board of Education* would gain him nationwide attention. He would come to know presidents, congressmen, world leaders, sports heroes, and religious figures. But Marshall never forgot the struggles of common people. They were the ones who kept him focused on what was important to him. He said:

> *As soon as I reach any town, I talk to the shoe-shine boys or the barbers or the people in the restaurants, because it's Mr. Joe Doakes who is very close to reality.*

Throughout his life, Marshall worked hard to bring freedom, justice, equality, and respect to all people, including blacks, women, the homeless, convicts, and the mentally ill. His work as a civil rights attorney often was dangerous, and he would narrowly escape death on more than one occasion. Later, as a federal judge, solicitor general of the United States, and U.S. Supreme Court justice, Marshall would be threatened with violence. But he would hold strong to his beliefs and not let threats prevent him from doing what he thought was right. He often joked about the threats in order to ease the tension, but he took them seriously.

Thurgood Marshall would achieve many things in his lifetime. But he always recognized that much more had to be done before all people were considered equal—in the eyes of their fellow citizens and in the eyes of the law. ✍

2 GROWING UP

❧⦿❧

When Thurgood Marshall was born in Baltimore, Maryland, on July 2, 1908, he was named Thoroughgood. He had a strong personality, and when he decided to do something, he didn't quit until it was accomplished. This determination and perseverance was evident early on. When he was ready to start elementary school, he announced he was tired of his long first name. He wanted to be called Thurgood—both at home and at school. He even convinced his mother to have it changed on his birth certificate.

Perhaps Thurgood got his strength from his father, Willie Marshall, who was never afraid to speak his mind. This trait, however, had caused him problems. As a child, Willie had dropped out of elementary school after talking back to his teachers

Theaters were often segregated, with separate entrances for black and white moviegoers.

Segregated water fountains were in use well into the 1930s and 1940s.

and principal. Unable to attend school, Willie worked in his father's grocery store until he earned enough money to move into his own home. Then he took a job as a porter, or luggage carrier, at Baltimore's railroad station.

Thurgood's mother, Norma, had graduated from high school. She had attended college at Coppin State in Baltimore to become a teacher. But before her college graduation, Norma discovered she was pregnant with Willie's baby. They married April 17, 1905. Norma went on to graduate from college and receive a teaching license. About five months after Willie and Norma married, a son, Aubrey, was born. Three years later, on July 2, 1908, Thurgood's birth completed the Marshall family.

Thurgood grew up in a violent time. The year he was born, 89 blacks were lynched. Riots caused by racial tension between blacks and whites plagued the country, especially the South. On August 14, 1908, when Thurgood was little more than a month old, riots broke out in Springfield, Illinois. Eight people were killed.

The Illinois riots were most disturbing, since many people didn't expect race riots in the North. Difficulties between blacks and whites dated back to before the Civil War (1861–1865), leading to racial tension in the South.

Blacks were tired of being treated as second-class citizens. Although blacks were legally free, the South's so-called Jim Crow laws forced them to live separate from whites. When blacks tried to challenge the Jim Crow laws, violence often followed.

As a boy, Thurgood was shielded from violence. However, they couldn't protect him from

The term Jim Crow was first heard in 1832 when comedian Thomas "Daddy" Rice performed the song "Jump Jim Crow" onstage. Rice, who was white, used makeup called blackface that made him appear to be black. His acting and singing mocked blacks and what he called their "comic" lifestyle. Soon, Jim Crow was used as a racial slur to refer to blacks in general. In the late 1800s, laws used to restrict blacks were called Jim Crow laws. These laws segregated everything from public bathrooms to parks and hospitals. Facilities for blacks were in much poorer condition than those for whites.

segregation. The Marshalls lived in a neighborhood on Druid Hill Avenue in the northwest section of Baltimore. This was ranked as the nicest of the three parts of town where blacks were allowed to live.

When Thurgood was 2, his family moved to the Harlem district of New York City. Norma Marshall's older sister Denmedia Dodson invited them to stay with her family. Dodson said Willie could find steady work with her husband, Clarence, as a waiter.

At the time, Harlem was a vibrant community with an exciting nightlife. Clubs and gambling brought in blacks and whites alike. Harlem proved to be a pleasant place for many black families to live, particularly those hoping to escape Jim Crow laws.

Thurgood at age 1.

However, New York wasn't free of racism either.

The Marshall family moved back to Baltimore in 1914 when Norma's mother needed help to recover from a broken leg. While the Marshalls had been gone, racial tensions had become worse in Baltimore. Some wealthy blacks had moved into homes that were in once all-white areas, and politicians in favor of segregation wanted it stopped.

Those working for integration found themselves powerless to stop the passing of a city law that separated black neighborhoods from white ones. The law was later ruled illegal in court, but other forms of prejudice continued. Some Baltimore stores did not allow blacks. When Thurgood started school, he had to go to a school designed for blacks.

Thurgood's school was the best one that black children could attend in the city. But it still wasn't as good as the schools for white children. It even ended early so black children could start picking strawberries when they were ripe in the spring.

The Marshall family lived in a nice neighborhood with Norma's brother, Fearless Mentor Williams, and his wife, Flo. Many people who lived in the area were black, but one neighbor was Jewish, and others were Russian, Italian, and German immigrants.

Fearless and Flo had no children and enjoyed spending time with their nephews. Thurgood looked up to his uncle, who worked as a personal attendant to the president of the B&O Railroad. Fearless knew many of the city's white politicians and business leaders.

By the time he was 7 years old, Thurgood was working at a local grocery store owned by a kind Jewish man whom he knew only as Mr. Hale.

Thurgood earned 10 cents a day delivering groceries in his wagon. Sometimes the Hale family came to Fearless and Flo's home for dinner. Thurgood did not realize how rare it was in those days for a white family to share a meal at a black family's home. To Thurgood, it was everyday life. In fact, Thurgood and Hale's son Sammy became best friends.

Thurgood's sheltered life came to an end in 1919. Many blacks, including Thurgood's uncles, had fought for the United States military during World War I. When the war ended in 1918, many black veterans came home to a different kind of war. In the summer

Black soldiers found it hard to adjust to racial tension when they returned from the war.

of 1919, race riots broke out across the country between white segregationists and black veterans, who were being treated as second-class citizens.

One of the bloodiest riots broke out in Washington, D.C., only 40 miles (64 kilometers) south of Baltimore. It made a lasting impression on 11-year-old Thurgood. The riot was sparked by a July 19 headline in the *Washington Post:* "Negroes Attack Girl ... White Men Vainly Pursue." Earlier that month, the National Association for the Advancement of Colored People (NAACP) wrote letters to Washington's largest newspapers complaining that sensational headlines fanned the flames of racial tension.

The "attack" to which the headline referred was an incident where two black sailors grabbed an umbrella from a woman and insulted her. The woman was upset but unharmed. About 200 white sailors set out to find the two black sailors. They wanted to lynch them. The streets of southwest Washington were searched, and any blacks who were found were beaten. The violence continued for two more nights. On the third night, heavy rain and 2,000 federal troops finally brought the violence to an end.

Thurgood heard about the riots. He was shocked that black military veterans would be attacked. He sadly realized that even heroes—black heroes—weren't protected from hatred and violence at the hands of racists. ✑

3 LIFE'S LESSONS

❦

By 1921, 12-year-old Thurgood and his 15-year-old brother, Aubrey, were old enough to be somewhat independent, so their mother went back to school. She wanted to become a full-time kindergarten teacher. She completed her education in 1921, but getting a job was difficult. She took substitute teaching jobs wherever she could find them.

Norma and Willie pushed Aubrey and Thurgood to do their best. Willie always felt it was his lack of education that limited him to jobs as a porter or a waiter. He wanted more for his sons, and he expected them to get good grades.

Thurgood had not always taken his education seriously. He was popular with the other students, and he often clowned around and teased the girls.

Although Thurgood Marshall was a good student, he still enjoyed joking and laughing with his fellow classmates.

But when he entered the seventh grade, he decided to work harder. His extra effort paid off. Thurgood did so well that school officials moved him up to the eighth grade that year.

In 1921, Thurgood started high school at the Colored High and Training School, Baltimore's first high school for black students. The school did not measure up to the city's white schools. It had fewer books and less equipment. There was no library, gym, or cafeteria. So many students crowded into the school that the principal was forced to divide them into two groups. One group went to school in the morning, the other in the afternoon.

From his second-floor classroom, Thurgood

A view of Light Street near Pier One, Baltimore, in 1924

could see the Northwest Baltimore Police Station. He often found himself looking out the window and watching the prisoners—most of them black—file into the station. On many occasions, Thurgood heard them being questioned or saw them being beaten. To make Thurgood pay attention, his teachers often had to tell him to pull down the window shades.

Although Thurgood had become more serious about his studies, he still had a mischievous side. When he ended up in the school office, Thurgood knew what his punishment would be—banishment to the basement with a copy of the U.S. Constitution. He couldn't return to class until he had memorized a section of the constitution. "Before I left that school, I knew the whole thing by heart," Thurgood recalled.

He also learned about the law from his father. Willie liked to visit local courtrooms and watch trial proceedings. When he came home, he told Thurgood stories about the cases.

Despite their busy schedules, the Marshalls usually found time to eat dinner together as a family. Thurgood later recalled:

> We lived on a respectable street, but behind us were back alleys where roughnecks and the tough kids hung out. When it was time for dinner, my mother used to go to the front door to call my older brother. Then she'd go to the back door and call me.

After dinner, Thurgood, Aubrey, and their father often engaged in heated conversations about the day's events. In debates with his sons, Willie used tactics he learned from the lawyers in court. "I got the idea of being a lawyer from arguing with my dad," Thurgood said. "We'd argue about everything."

Thurgood was chosen for a spot on the high school debate team. During his first year, he became the group's main debater and captain. He was a natural leader, directing others to do more research on points he felt needed strengthening. He also served on the student council and class treasury committee.

Cab Calloway led one of America's most famous bands that included jazz legends Ben Webster and Dizzy Gillespie.

Thurgood was smart, good looking, had a great sense of humor, and told good stories. He attracted a lot of friends—both boys and girls. Among them was Anita Short, a girl on his debate team. They usually ate lunch together, and he often walked her home after school. One of Thurgood's good friends was Cab Calloway, who would go on to become a famous jazz singer and band leader.

In 1924, Thurgood's father

became ill and could not work. Aubrey was in college, and the Marshalls fell behind on his tuition payments. Norma started working as a playground director to supplement her salary as a substitute teacher. Frustrated by his inability to work and lack of education, Willie began to heavily abuse alcohol.

To help out his family, Thurgood worked part time as a porter for the B&O Railroad, his father's former job. As Thurgood got closer to his high school graduation, his parents wondered if they could afford his college tuition. Norma pressed Thurgood to work hard and finish school a semester early. He could use that extra time to work and save money for college.

He graduated early, and in February 1925, he began working full time as a railroad dining car waiter. He quickly learned how unfairly black workers were treated compared to whites. For example, blacks couldn't join labor unions like whites could. The unions helped their members get higher wages and better working conditions. If blacks even suggested joining labor unions, they were fired. Blacks also weren't paid for extra time they worked. Thurgood

By the early 1930s, most Americans knew the name Cab Calloway. Although he started law school, he quit to follow his passion for singing and dancing. He became a celebrated jazz entertainer. For years, he and his bands played in New York City's Cotton Club, one of the most famous jazz clubs in history. Calloway died in 1994.

learned to quietly do his work so he wouldn't lose his job. In six months, he earned enough to pay one year's college tuition.

While at Lincoln University, Marshall (second row, second from right) joined a fraternity. He was such a troublemaker that he was kicked out of the university twice for his pranks.

In September, Thurgood Marshall started classes at Lincoln University in Oxford, Pennsylvania. However, he spent more time playing cards with his friends than studying. He made many friends and got good enough grades to pass his classes. He also joined the debate team and took a job on campus baking bread in the school cafeteria.

Although Lincoln University accepted only black

students, all of the teachers were white. This made Marshall think more about segregation. In one of his classes, the students voted on whether the school should also hire black teachers. The majority, including Marshall, voted to keep the faculty all white. A student named Langston Hughes couldn't believe how his classmates had voted. He called for a campuswide vote. However, the results were the same. Students gave many reasons for wanting an all-white teaching staff. Some said they didn't want any changes because they thought that things were already running smoothly. Others believed students would not respect black teachers.

Langston Hughes went on to be a world-famous writer whose written work was strongly influenced by jazz music. He used his gift of writing to make people aware of how minorities were being treated. He published 16 books of poems, two novels, eight children's books, two history books, and countless other works to help bring equality to all people. He died on May 22, 1967.

Not long after the campus vote, Marshall and some of his friends went to a movie in Oxford. Since the theater was a segregated facility, the usher told the black students to sit in the balcony. Angry that they were being treated unfairly, Marshall and his friends asked for their money back. The usher refused. Before leaving, the young men pulled down the theater's curtains and broke the front door.

News of the incident quickly traveled around

Langston Hughes spent six months touring Europe and west Africa before attending Lincoln University.

campus. Hughes confronted Marshall. How could he get so upset over not being able to sit where he wanted in a movie theater but still vote against giving black people a chance to teach at his college? Hughes made Marshall think hard about racial issues. They started meeting together, and in time, Marshall realized how unfair the Jim Crow laws were.

Hughes graduated in 1929, but Marshall had one more year of college. During that year, Marshall worked hard to integrate the college teaching staff. He argued to the students that getting a college degree meant nothing if it didn't qualify them to come back to their own school and teach. Many students listened to Marshall, and another vote was taken on the issue. This time, they voted to integrate the faculty. The following year, the university hired its first black professor.

Marshall was also working on his personal life. The 21-year-old college senior had fallen in love with Vivian Burey, a 17-year-old freshman at the University of Pennsylvania. They married on September 4, 1929.

After the wedding, Marshall went back to Lincoln to finish his education, while Vivian lived in Baltimore with Marshall's parents. Marshall studied hard during the next four months. In January 1930, he graduated with honors.

After graduation, Marshall took a job as an insurance agent. The job paid his bills, but he found it so boring that he went back to working as a waiter. He planned to save as much money as he could so he could go to law school. His mother always dreamed that her son Aubrey would be a doctor and that Thurgood would be a dentist or a lawyer. Aubrey was now in medical school. The Marshalls hoped they could figure out a way to pay for both Aubrey and Thurgood's educations. Norma wanted her sons to be able to get an education in whatever field they wanted. Thurgood promised to work hard through the summer to help pay for his tuition. ॐ

4 LAW SCHOOL AND THE NAACP

☙❧

The University of Maryland Law School was just a few blocks from Marshall's home in Baltimore. Tuition rates were low, and it had a good reputation as a public school that educated its students well. Marshall very much wanted to go there, but he didn't bother to apply. The school made turning away blacks a common practice. Marshall did not think he would be any different from other black students who had tried to go there.

Some law schools in the North admitted blacks, but Marshall couldn't afford their higher tuitions. Marshall was accepted at the Howard University Law School in Washington, D.C. While this school admitted blacks, it was not known for attracting the best students. This made Marshall angry. He wanted to get an education, but a degree from a school with a poor reputation might not mean much. But there was no way he would be allowed to attend the University of Maryland. Howard was his only choice.

As fall approached, Marshall realized that he didn't have enough money for tuition. He planned to work another year and save more money, but his mother wouldn't hear of it. She pawned her wedding rings to make sure her son had money for law school.

The University of Maryland was founded in 1856 as the Maryland Agricultural College. The first female students enrolled in 1916. Black students were not admitted until 1951.

Marshall could not afford to live in Washington, D.C., so he rode to school every day from Baltimore. He got up very early so he could leave at 5 A.M. and walk to the railroad station.

On the first day of classes, the new dean, Charles Hamilton Houston, announced to the students that there were now stricter standards at Howard University. Houston was determined to improve the school's reputation. It would be recognized for excellence, and any student who wasn't committed to studying law would be weeded out. Houston predicted that two-thirds of the freshman class would fail their first year. Marshall was happy with the new standards of excellence and was determined not to be one of the students who would fail.

Marshall studied on the train to and from school and became the top student in his class. His hard work qualified him for a job as student assistant in the school's law library. Along with providing some extra cash, the job allowed Marshall to work with Houston. The two soon developed a close bond. Marshall often stayed at school until 10 P.M. By the time he got home, he was too tired to do anything but sleep. In the morning, he would again walk to the train station and catch a train to school. Marshall recalled:

Charles Hamilton Houston was a strong leader even before becoming dean of Howard University Law School. After serving as an Army officer during World War I, he returned home to get more education. In the fall of 1919, Houston started classes at Harvard Law School. He became the first black editor of the Harvard Law Review and the primary force behind the NAACP's decision to attack discrimination in public schools.

Charles Hamilton Houston would become Marshall's mentor and close friend.

When I was in law school, in my first year I lost thirty pounds solely from work. Intellectual work, studying. And that's how you get ahead of people.

As part of their education, Houston took his students to police stations, jails, the attorney general's office, and anywhere else they might learn more about the law. Marshall took advantage of his free time by visiting the U.S. Supreme Court, where he watched lawyers argue cases in front of the highest judges in the nation.

In 1932, 24-year-old Marshall started his final year of law school. Houston allowed his top students to work on real cases. Marshall helped defend George Crawford, a black man facing the death penalty in Virginia. Crawford was accused of killing two white women. While Crawford admitted to trying to rob the women, he said he didn't kill them.

Marshall worked hard on the case. He did everything from fetching coffee to researching legal matters. He loved learning from Houston. The way

Houston worked made him realize that a black man really could make a difference in the lives of others. Crawford was depending on Houston to save his life.

Crawford's jury consisted of 12 white men. At the end of the trial, the jurors found Crawford guilty, but he didn't receive the death penalty. For Marshall and Houston, this was a huge victory. Marshall said:

> *If you get a life term for a Negro charged with killing a white person in Virginia, you've won. You've won because normally they were hanging them.*

Marshall graduated with a law degree from Howard in June 1933. He was at the top of his class academically. Yet getting a job wouldn't be easy. No white Baltimore law firms hired black attorneys. The few black lawyers in town worked alone. So Marshall decided to work as a waiter again, save some money, and ponder his future.

The U.S. Supreme Court is the only court in the nation that is referred to in the U.S. Constitution. The Supreme Court's responsibility is to make sure all levels of government act according to the Constitution and the laws passed by Congress. The court has nine members—a chief justice and eight associate justices. There is no higher court to which a case can go. Not every case brought to the court is heard by the justices. Since it would be impossible to consider all cases, the Supreme Court chooses to hear those cases that it believes to be most important.

But Houston had a different job for him. The NAACP was planning to challenge whether segregation was legal in public schools. Members wanted more information about the situation in the schools. They hired Houston and Marshall to go to Southern schools and find out what they were like.

The duo traveled in Houston's car. Because Jim Crow laws barred blacks from staying in hotels or eating in restaurants, they stayed in private homes. They ate wherever they could buy food.

The condition of some of the black schools they visited shocked Marshall. In some cases, huge patches of sky could be seen through holes in the roofs. Often, the schools had dirt floors, which turned

Schools for black children in the South were often little more than old wooden buildings.

to mud when it rained. "Conditions were much worse than we heard they were," Marshall said.

In Mississippi, they visited a run-down school surrounded by shacks where black sharecroppers lived. As Houston examined the school, Marshall sat down to eat lunch. While he was eating an orange, he noticed that a boy was watching him. Marshall held out an extra orange in his hand. The hungry boy quickly took it and began eating. "The kid did not even take the peeling off," Marshall said. "He had never seen an orange before. He just bit right through it and enjoyed it."

The experience he gained in the South gave Marshall the desire to make a difference in people's lives. He wanted to make the world a better place for people like the poor boy he met in Mississippi. Though he knew he'd have a hard time making a living as a black lawyer, Marshall felt this was the best way to help others. ✍

The Great Depression of the 1930s made it more difficult for people to feed their families.

5 STRUGGLING LAWYER

Marshall passed the Maryland bar exam on his first try. He was now an official, full-fledged lawyer. In the fall of 1933, he rented a small, one-room office in downtown Baltimore. He had a desk borrowed from a friend, a phone, and a rug that once had adorned his parents' living room floor.

Clients were hard to come by. People tended to hire white lawyers if they could afford them. Even black people at that time did not trust black lawyers with their cases because legal officials were often prejudiced against them.

Marshall handled several small cases, but the money he earned wasn't enough to pay his rent and other expenses. He tried to save money however he could. He usually brought sandwiches from home

Black schools in the South were often poorly attended until after the cotton harvest season was done.

Pallbearers in a parade carried a casket and a sign that reads "Here Lies Jim Crow." The NAACP grew quickly, from 9,000 members in 1917 to nearly 500,000 by 1946.

instead of going out for lunch. When he did receive a big fee from a client, he would celebrate by going out for steaks with his wife and friends.

Because he had only a few clients, Marshall had a lot of free time. He used this spare time to work with Houston on more assignments for the NAACP. Most of them involved further investigations of the conditions of black schools in the South.

In Mississippi, some serious threats from whites who wanted their town to remain segregated made Houston and Marshall fear for their lives. After that, the state leader of the NAACP provided a car with armed men to follow and protect the two lawyers.

While traveling from city to city, Marshall and Houston talked to people about integration. Houston believed that if black and white children went to the same school, they would get to know one another, and racial hatred would disappear. They would also receive an equal education. Both he and Marshall believed that was the key to equal rights.

The time Marshall spent away from home was difficult for his wife, Vivian. They still lived with Marshall's parents, and so did Aubrey and his family. The situation in the Marshall house was tense. As Willie's drinking problem grew worse, he became more difficult to live with. Norma tried to hold the family together, and Vivian kept busy working at a variety of jobs to help support the family.

In 1934, Marshall's law practice picked up a bit. He handled divorces, car accidents, and whatever else he could find. One of his most important cases was one he received through the NAACP. Marshall represented Virtis Lucas, a black man accused of killing a white man. After Marshall convinced an all-white jury that police had beaten a confession out of Lucas, the jurors found the defendant not guilty of murder and instead convicted him of manslaughter, which meant he hadn't planned to kill the man. He was sentenced to six months in jail. Officials at the NAACP were thrilled. The conviction on a lesser charge and a sentence of less than a year in prison proved that a black lawyer could defend a black client and get a white jury to listen.

Marshall also took on a case that would make

history. For the first time, a black lawyer defended a white client—Bernard Ades, a Maryland lawyer. Ades accused a judge of not giving his client a fair trial because his client was black. The judge, William Coleman, said the comment damaged his reputation and started a hearing in the state court against Ades to get Ades' license taken away. When Marshall and Houston were called to help Ades, Coleman threatened them and said that he would have them put in jail if they called him a racist in court.

Things got easier for Houston and Marshall when they found out that Coleman withdrew himself from the case to avoid a conflict of interest. The new judge assigned to the case scolded Ades for the comments he made but allowed him to keep his law license.

Marshall was getting a reputation for being a good lawyer. He worked long hours, often at the expense of spending time with his wife. But Marshall knew he had to work twice as hard as white lawyers to convince white judges and juries to listen to him. He tried to be as perfect as he possibly could. "I never filed a paper in any court with an erasure on it. If I changed a word, it had to be typed all over," Marshall said. Marshall discovered he could get along with most white judges—even those who gave other black lawyers a difficult time.

Marshall began using his legal skills to improve working conditions for blacks. He remembered his

The Bethlehem Steel Mill in Sparrows Point, Maryland, was financially devastated during the Great Depression of the 1930s.

days as a waiter for the railroad and how unfair it was that blacks could not join labor unions. When labor leaders asked him to help get black workers to join the union, he jumped at the chance. Marshall began meeting with black workers at Bethlehem Steel, one of Baltimore's biggest companies.

Most black workers didn't trust the white union leaders, but they did trust Marshall. He convinced them that joining a labor union was the best way to protect their rights as an employee. He even helped get a black man elected as the union's treasurer.

But not everyone liked what Marshall was doing. Leaders at Bethlehem Steel felt their control of the organization was being threatened. They hired thugs to break up meetings where Marshall was discussing cooperation between workers. On one occasion, Marshall was forced to run for his life when ruffians chased him from a meeting. Marshall recalled:

> *It was raining and we started running and two of us saw a church. It had a big hedge around it so we got down in the hedge and these guys were coming by shouting. … We lay down in the mud. At first, that mud was cold, but it got real warm. We stayed there until they left, after midnight.*

The NAACP would prove key to helping the Marshalls with their financial obligations.

Despite his growing reputation as a good lawyer, Marshall still struggled to support his family. By the summer of 1936, he was getting overdue notices on his bills. His brother, Aubrey, had been unable to work, and his father had gotten fired from his job

after an argument with a white employee. Marshall needed to make more money.

Houston knew the struggles Marshall faced. He also recognized the young lawyer's skills. Houston often traveled around the country raising money for the NAACP. Now he suggested that Marshall run the New York office while he was gone.

Houston wrote a note to Walter White, head of the NAACP:

> You would not be able to find a more faithful person than Thurgood or a more dependable office man. But I am afraid he is just not the type to make a success in private practice. He needs to be in a school or on a salary where he could work to his heart's content in the exhausting way he likes to work, without financial worry. He is perhaps too conscientious and painstaking to be a commercial suffering lawyer.

Born July 1, 1893, in Atlanta, Georgia, Walter White served as executive secretary of the NAACP from 1931 until his death in 1955. With blond hair and blue eyes, White easily could have passed as a white man, but he chose to live as a black. A leader for civil rights, White fought for laws that would make lynching illegal. He promoted equality for all black people. He was awarded the NAACP's top honor, the Spingarn Medal, in 1937.

White agreed to give the young lawyer a chance. Marshall and his wife, Vivian, packed up their belongings and moved to New York City, where a full-time job with the NAACP office awaited him.

6 FIGHTING FOR EQUALITY

❧⟨∞⟩❧

In 1936, Houston and Marshall began sharing an office at the NAACP building in New York. The two made quite a pair. Though by now they were the best of friends, they could not have been more different. Forty-one-year-old Houston always looked professional. He was well-groomed, and his suits were neat. Marshall's clothes, on the other hand, were usually wrinkled by the end of the workday, and his shirttails often hung out. His loud, booming voice and laugh often could be heard throughout the building as he told humorous stories to co-workers.

Houston drove his staff members hard and expected their work to be perfect. Twenty-eight-year-old Marshall worked hard to please Houston and was more than willing to learn from the older, more

The NAACP hung a banner outside its headquarters in New York every time a man was lynched.

experienced attorney who had become his mentor. The two worked well together.

One of Marshall's first cases as a full-time lawyer for the NAACP involved school teachers' salaries. White teachers were paid more than black teachers. It was a subject Marshall knew well. His mother had always made less than white teachers who did the same job. In some cases, black teachers earned about half of what white teachers made.

African-American school children protested the Norfolk school board's treatment of black teachers.

George Fox, superintendent of the Anne Arundel County school district in Maryland, justified the difference in pay by saying that even the worst white

teacher was better than the best black teacher. This made Marshall angry, but he knew he had to hold his temper in order to win his case. Marshall found a school principal, Walter Mills, who would help him challenge this inequality in court. Marshall proved that Fox was not qualified to judge teaching talent and that he was a racist. The judge agreed.

The impact of Marshall's victory went far beyond this one Maryland school district. The Maryland state legislature realized that if other school districts in the state were challenged with the same issue, they would also lose. Each lawsuit would cost the state a great deal of money. To avoid further lawsuits, the state legislature passed a law establishing a standard pay scale for all teachers, regardless of their race. Marshall was thrilled with his success, and he began filing similar lawsuits in other states. He won most of the cases.

Marshall also began taking cases involving voting rights and blacks being charged unfairly with crimes. He and Houston kept looking for more ways they could challenge segregation in schools. The Supreme Court had ruled that separate schools for black and white children were acceptable if the buildings were equal. As Houston and Marshall had already seen, schools for blacks were often shacks compared to the schools for whites. Houston believed that lawsuits demanding equal facilities would end segregation in a roundabout way. School districts would not be able to afford to build nice, new schools for blacks, and they would have to let blacks and whites attend the same schools.

In July 1938, Houston decided to leave the NAACP, and Marshall had to handle the legal work alone. The following year, the NAACP established the Legal Defense Fund (LDF), and Marshall was asked to head it up. The purpose of the LDF was described in its charter:

In 1896, the U.S. Supreme Court ruled on a case called Plessy v. Ferguson. *In the ruling, the court said that states could not prohibit segregation on public transportation, such as railroad cars, streetcars, or steamboats. The Supreme Court's ruling became the foundation for Jim Crow laws, which kept blacks from using the same water fountains, restrooms, restaurants, and other public facilities that whites used. The Court has never officially overruled* Plessy v. Ferguson.

> *To render free legal aid to Negroes who suffer legal injustice because of their race or color and cannot afford to employ legal assistance. To seek and promote educational opportunities denied to Negroes because of their color. To conduct research and publish information on educational facilities and inequalities furnished for Negroes out of public funds and on the status of the Negro in American life.*

The LDF received more requests for legal help than it could handle. Marshall did what he could, but sometimes he had to help people find other lawyers in their area. But one case he could not pass up involved two blacks charged with attempted murder during a riot in Columbia, Tennessee. The riot had started on February 26, 1946. A black woman named Gladys Stephenson and her son James had paid to have a radio fixed, but when they picked it up it was still broken. When they told repairman Billy Fleming about it, he claimed that the radio had been fixed and that Gladys must have broken it again. When Gladys said that wasn't true, Fleming slapped her and pushed her out of his store. Defending his mother, James punched Fleming and knocked him through the store's window.

When police arrived on the scene, they sided with Fleming, who was taken to the hospital. Gladys and James were handcuffed and taken to jail. As news of the incident spread through the town, an angry white mob formed outside the police station. Worried for the Stephensons' safety, the sheriff contacted two black leaders from the community and asked them to sneak the Stephensons out of town. The sheriff was afraid they might be lynched.

People living in the black section of Columbia were afraid the mob might attack them. They armed themselves and shot out streetlights to discourage the mob from coming into their neighborhood at night. The sheriff knew the danger these black citizens were in, and he ordered police officers to stand guard around the perimeter of the neighborhood to watch for signs of violence.

The situation seemed to be under control until some of the officers drove their police cars into the black neighborhood. Afraid that white mob members were in the cars, some frightened blacks began shooting. The white mob came running at the sound of gunfire. A riot had begun.

Vandalism during the 1946 race riots caused damage to a drugstore as well as to many other stores and residences in Columbia, Tennessee.

Eventually, about 500 National Guardsmen and 100 state troopers descended on the area in an effort to bring peace to Columbia again. But they also caused a lot of damage. They chopped down doors with axes, broke shop windows, and tossed out

people's furniture. They claimed they were looking for weapons and hidden gunmen.

Police shot and killed two blacks they said were trying to escape. Not everyone believed the claim. More than 100 others were arrested, and several of them were charged with murder. The black community in Columbia knew they needed help. They called the NAACP.

Marshall found lawyers to defend several of the people who were arrested. He defended two of them himself. Their trial ended on November 18 after four days. The jury found William Pillow not guilty but convicted Lloyd Kennedy and sentenced him to five years in jail. After the verdicts were read, Marshall got into a car owned by black lawyer Alexander Looby and headed to Nashville to plan Kennedy's appeal. Because of the racial tension in Columbia, they had been staying in Nashville, where they felt safer. However, that day they wouldn't get very far.

As Marshall, Looby, and the rest of the lawyers approached the edge of town, they were stopped by Columbia police officers and state highway patrolmen. The officers ordered Marshall into the back of an unmarked police car and told his friends to leave town. Fearful for Marshall's life, Looby ignored the order and followed the unmarked car. The car turned off the main highway onto a dirt road. They stopped at the river, where police again told them to leave, and again Looby and the others refused. Finally, the police officers gave up and turned around to drive Marshall back to town.

His friends' courage and stubbornness likely saved Marshall's life. From the backseat of the police car, Marshall saw an angry mob waiting along the riverbank. If his friends had not followed the police car down the dark country road, Marshall most likely would have been lynched.

Marshall was still not out of danger. He and his friends made plans to quickly leave Columbia in a different car. Someone drove Looby's car in another direction. It was used as a decoy to make the mob follow the wrong car. Marshall remembered:

> *And sure enough, the mob was coming around the corner when we left. So they followed Looby's car, which we'd hoped they'd do. And incidentally, when they found out that I wasn't in it, they beat the driver bad enough that he was in the hospital for a week.*

In spite of the risks, Marshall kept working on Kennedy's case. The appeals court eventually reduced Kennedy's sentence from five years to 10 months. The Stephensons were never charged with any crime in the incident.

Marshall's hard work in attempting to eliminate

The first Spingarn Medal was awarded in 1915. Since then, there has been a recipient every year except 1938. Marshall was honored by the NAACP in 1946.

discrimination was rewarded. In 1946, he received the Spingarn Medal, which the NAACP awards annually for outstanding achievement by a black American.

Throughout his career, Marshall challenged the law that kept blacks from buying homes in white neighborhoods. He questioned the military and charged it with treating black soldiers differently from white soldiers. Across the country, Marshall fought to integrate colleges. One of his biggest cases involved Ada Sipuel, a black woman who wanted to attend the University of Oklahoma Law School. She was refused admission because of her race. Marshall took her case all the way to the U.S. Supreme Court. In January 1948, the court ruled in Sipuel's favor, but the battle wasn't done.

The Supreme Court ruled Sipuel could attend the University of Oklahoma Law School because no similar program existed for blacks in the area. But Oklahoma lawmakers still found a way to keep Sipuel out of the university. They created a new law school for blacks—the Langston Law School, which was located in the state Capitol building. They hired three law professors and told Sipuel that she had to apply for admission at Langston.

Marshall went back to the Supreme Court for help. He wanted the court to force the University of Oklahoma to admit Sipuel. However, the Supreme Court decided the new school for blacks created new issues. Marshall would have to take his case back to the lower courts. Marshall refused to give up. He explained to the lower court that the Langston Law School was a sham. He argued that blacks suffered when they were not educated with white students going into the same profession. But Marshall could not convince the judge, and he lost his case.

Before Marshall had a chance to appeal the case to a higher court, the university gave in and admitted Sipuel. She started classes two weeks late, and the white students in her class welcomed her.

Marshall (center) watched Ada Lois Sipuel apply to the University of Oklahoma Law School.

They offered her books and notes to help her catch up. School officials were not as kind, however. They forced her to sit in the back of the classrooms under a sign that read "COLORED." Sipuel studied hard and did well in school, and by her second semester, the "COLORED" signs were removed. Sipuel began sitting in the front row.

By 1950, Marshall had quite a good reputation. With 10 Supreme Court victories, he was considered the top civil rights expert in the nation. But his biggest case was yet to come. ✒

7 BROWN V. BOARD OF EDUCATION

೭⊙⋊⊙ꝰ

Thurgood Marshall had been successful in his fight against segregation in colleges. Now he wanted to end segregation in all public schools. Always open to the ideas of others, Marshall called a conference of lawyers in New York City. He let them argue about the best ways to attack segregation while he sat back and listened.

The lawyers convinced Marshall to argue that segregation, for any reason, was wrong. Marshall agreed and planned to prove that segregation made black children feel less important than white students. But before he could take the issue to court, he had to find people who were brave enough to be the plaintiffs in the case. They had to be willing to challenge segregation in their school districts.

Marshall stood on the steps of the Supreme Court building before hearing the results of Brown v. Board of Education.

Many parents thought they would lose their jobs or their children would be harmed if they dared to fight segregation.

In South Carolina, Marshall found 19 parents who were willing to sue for complete school integration. The trial began in Charleston on May 28, 1951. More than 500 people tried to pack into the 75-seat courtroom. People came from miles around to catch a glimpse of Thurgood Marshall.

When the trial started, Marshall was caught off guard. The attorney for the state of South Carolina readily admitted that schools for black children weren't equal to those for whites. A shocked Marshall didn't know what to do. He had spent so much time finding witnesses and evidence to prove the schools weren't equal. Now the state was flatly admitting it.

The proceedings could have ended right there, but

Hearings about public school desegregation drew large crowds of spectators.

one of the judges added that one point in Marshall's court documents still needed to be addressed. Before the state went to the effort of making black schools equal to white schools, the court needed to decide whether segregation was constitutional. Marshall quickly came up with a new strategy. He presented witnesses who would say that segregation was harmful to black children's self-esteem, or the way they thought about themselves.

On the witness stand, Dr. David Krech, a psychologist from Harvard University in Cambridge, Massachusetts, testified:

> *Legal segregation hampers the mental, emotional, physical and financial development of colored children and aggravates the very prejudices from which it arises. Damage if continued for ten or twelve years will be permanent.*

The lawyer for South Carolina argued that it wasn't a school's responsibility to worry about the development of children's personalities or how they felt about themselves. He added that integrating schools, or mixing black and white children in the classroom, would lead to violence. He said that in time, the violence would force South Carolina to quit offering public education. In the end, the judges voted 2-1 in favor of the state. Marshall lost his case.

Around the same time, Marshall was working on another school segregation case—*Brown v. Board of Education of Topeka, Kansas*. Marshall assigned two of his lawyers to the case. The lawyers argued that separate schools could never be equal, that segregation always meant inequality, and that there was another problem with segregation. In Topeka, black students were forced to travel long distances to black schools instead of attending white schools that were much closer to their homes. Again, however, the judges ruled against the plaintiff. Marshall and the NAACP had lost another case.

Children involved with Brown v. Board of Education *were (from left) Vicki Henderson, Donald Henderson, Linda Brown, James Emanuel, Nancy Todd, and Katherine Carper.*

Marshall appealed both cases, and they went all the way to U.S. Supreme Court. The Supreme Court justices decided to hear similar cases from other states at the same time. All the cases would be mixed together into one and collectively called *Brown v. Board of Education*. But it would be about a year before that would happen. Waiting was difficult for Marshall. He got little sleep and became grumpy. His personal life suffered as he concentrated on nothing but the Supreme Court case.

Again, Marshall gathered the great legal minds of the day and listened to how they would argue the case. In the end, though, the decision was his. Influenced by a study by psychologist Kenneth Clark, Marshall believed segregation prevented black children from achieving their full potential. This affected their entire lives, including the kinds of jobs they could get as adults. Because of this, separate schools could never be equal.

> *The plaintiffs in* Brown v. Board of Education *were Oliver Brown and 12 other parents. Brown's daughter Linda had to walk six blocks down a busy city street and cross train tracks to reach a bus stop that had no shelter from the weather. After that, it was a 30-minute bus ride to Monroe Elementary. Brown wanted Linda to go to Charles Sumner Elementary, only a few blocks from their house. Because it was an all-white school, Linda was denied enrollment. The NAACP convinced Brown and the other parents to fight for integration in Topeka's schools.*

Social psychologist Kenneth Clark designed a test to study if segregation affected black children. Four dolls, identical except for their skin color, were shown to a group of black children. The children were asked to pick the doll they liked best. Most picked the white dolls and thought the other dolls "looked bad." They were then given pictures of boys and girls and asked to color them the same color as themselves. Children with dark complexions colored the figures with white or yellow crayons. Clark concluded that prejudice, discrimination, and segregation caused black children to feel inferior and self-hatred.

Oral arguments, or spoken presentations of the case by both parties to the judge, were set to begin on December 9, 1952. Though Marshall's wife, Vivian, had been feeling ill for some time, she made the trip to Washington, D.C. She wanted to see this historic case.

The attorney for South Carolina argued that states had the right to segregate students if they wished. Marshall said that states' rights were not the issue. The rights of individuals were being violated by segregation. Marshall said that under the 14th Amendment to the Constitution, each citizen was guaranteed equal protection under the law, but equal protection was trampled by segregation.

After the arguments were completed, the Supreme Court's nine justices considered all they had heard. They debated the issue among themselves for months. However, they couldn't reach a decision. Most of the justices felt that such an important decision had to be unanimous or the public would never accept it. In an unusual move, the justices decided they needed more information and sent some questions to lawyers on both sides of the issue. They asked: Does the Supreme Court have the power to abolish school segregation? How would integration occur, if that was the court's decision?

In November 1953, the NAACP hired a group of experts, including Kenneth Clark, to prepare a 256-page paper answering the court's questions. Marshall stated that the only way the Supreme Court could allow segregation to continue was if the justices truly believed blacks were inferior to whites.

On December 7, the Supreme Court gathered to hear responses to their questions in person. For two days, the justices listened to both sides. Marshall ended his response by saying that the only reason for segregation was to keep people who once lived in slavery as close to that state as possible. Looking at the justices' faces, Marshall believed he had made a positive impact with that statement. He felt hopeful that they would side with him.

Again, the justices took time to consider all they had heard. While awaiting their decision, Marshall traveled around the country giving speeches at NAACP fund-raisers. The costs to the NAACP for the *Brown v. Board of Education* case were mounting. The expenses incurred because of the 256-page brief alone were about $40,000.

Marshall was in Mobile, Alabama, when he got a phone call telling him to come to Washington, D.C. The Supreme Court had reached its decision. On May 17, 1954, the court ruled unanimously that segregation was illegal and that separate educational facilities are not equal. Marshall and his team of lawyers won their case.

Marshall paused on the steps of the Supreme Court building so reporters could take his picture. Then he quickly made his way to the airport to catch a flight back to New York. At his office, Marshall celebrated the victory with his staff, friends, and reporters. Champagne corks popped, and laughter

George E.C. Hayes (left), Thurgood Marshall (center) and James M. Nabrit stand in front of the Supreme Court building.

filled the rooms. Marshall would remember this celebration as the best one he ever had.

Later, the group adjourned to one of Marshall's favorite restaurants where the festivities continued. When he heard some say the work of the NAACP was now done, Marshall offered these words of caution: "I don't want any of you to fool yourselves, it's just begun, the fight has just begun."

Opposition to the court's ruling went on for years. But Marshall and the NAACP continued to use the court system to fight against those who stood in the way of integration. At a Freedom Fund dinner in 1959, Marshall expressed his feelings about the opposition to integration:

> *It was hoped, but not expected, that the decisions in these cases would have settled "the problem." This, of course, as subsequent events proved, was hoping for too much. ... Opposition in areas of the South has ranged from violence, killings, and lynchings to economic boycotts and threats of violence. ... While our struggle has been one within the law, with honor and supported by both the constitutional law and the moral law of our civilization, the opposition in these state officials and others has been a disgrace to our democratic ideals, our country, our religious and every other principle of ethics or simple democracy.*

Marshall had won a great victory in court, but his personal life had its problems. His wife, Vivian, was dying of cancer. She had not told her husband about it until it was too late for him to try to help her. Vivian died on February 11, 1955, her 44th birthday.

Though he had concentrated more on his career than his marriage, Marshall had loved his wife. Her death came as quite a blow. To friends, Marshall seemed very depressed, and he lost a great deal of weight. For the first time in his life, he decided he needed to take a long vacation, and he went to Mexico to heal his broken heart.

Friends at the NAACP helped Marshall recover from his loss. Among them was his secretary, Cecilia "Cissy" Suyat who was Filipino-Hawaiian. Marshall and Cissy eventually fell in love and married on December 17, 1955. Cissy was able to give Marshall something he desperately wanted—children.

In 1956, Thurgood Jr. was born. Two years later, the Marshalls welcomed another son, John, to their family. Marshall was traveling less now and spending more time with his family. He had always loved toy trains, and now he had two sons with whom he could enjoy them.

By the end of the 1950s, Marshall found himself more distant from the black activists in the civil rights movement. Some of them, such as the Nation of Islam, even threatened him, claiming he was

Marshall with Cecilia and sons John and Thurgood Jr. at home in 1961

too close to whites. The Nation of Islam wanted to establish a black nation and keep blacks and whites separate—the opposite of what Marshall wanted.

Marshall was not fond of these people, nor was he fond of Martin Luther King Jr. He saw King's efforts at peaceful resistance as rather silly. Marshall did not think they would do any good. He still felt that the best way to change the country and gain equality for all was through the court system.

Through the years, Marshall gained a solid reputation in the United States as well as overseas. He was asked to come to Kenya to help write the country's constitution. The African nation had been

Martin Luther King Jr. was a Baptist minister from Montgomery, Alabama, who led the civil rights movement from the 1950s until his assassination in 1968. Known for his passionate speeches, King worked for change through nonviolence. In 1964, he won the Nobel Peace Prize for his efforts. Today, his birthday is celebrated as a national holiday—making him only the third American to receive such an honor. The first was President George Washington and the second was President Abraham Lincoln.

ruled by Great Britain since 1895. In 1963, it gained its independence and needed help setting up its own government and laws. Marshall accepted. Soon Kenya had its own president and National Assembly ready to create the nation's laws.

When he returned to the United States, Marshall discovered a crisis at home. Several black students had staged sit-ins at segregated restaurants in the South. Following King's idea of peaceful resistance, the students went to whites-only lunch counters and asked to be served. Restaurant owners called police, and the students were jailed. Many of the students' anxious parents called Marshall. They wanted his help to get their children out of jail.

At first, Marshall wasn't sure what to do. Historically, courts had sided with store owners. The courts said owners had the right to refuse service to anyone they chose. However, Marshall looked again at the 14th Amendment. He thought he could argue the part that allowed equal protection under the law. Marshall explained:

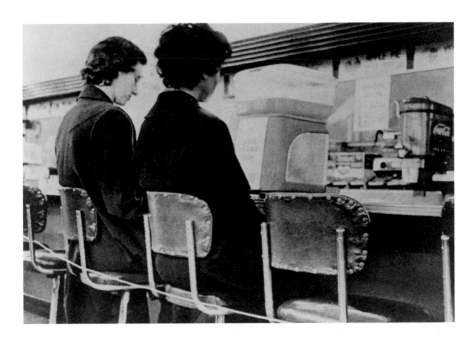

Once a store is opened to the public it means it is open to everybody—without discrimination.

Women protested segregation at a lunch counter in Nashville, Tennessee, in 1960.

The Supreme Court agreed. It ruled in favor of Marshall and the students. The Jim Crow laws were crumbling. And Marshall was about to take on another challenge—this time as a judge. ✍

73

8 ON THE FEDERAL STAGE

~~~⟨❦⟩~~~

In 1961, President John F. Kennedy nominated Thurgood Marshall for a position as a federal judge. On October 23, 1961, Marshall was sworn in as a judge of the U.S. Second Circuit Court of Appeals. This court heard appeals cases from lower courts in New York, Vermont, and Connecticut. It was a landmark appointment—Marshall became the first black judge to serve on the Second Circuit.

After his action-filled work on segregation and civil rights, Marshall didn't find serving as an appeals judge very satisfying. As a judge, he mainly dealt with big business issues, such as large corporations that were suing each other. But Marshall wouldn't sit on the court for long.

In July 1965, Marshall received a phone call from

Thurgood Marshall was sworn in as U.S. solicitor general with President Lyndon B. Johnson and his wife Cecilia at his side.

Lyndon Baines Johnson worked as a teacher before finding himself drawn into politics. Born on a farm in central Texas in 1908, Johnson attended Southwest Texas State Teachers College until he ran out of money. He taught school for a year in Cotulla, Texas, and saved his money so he could return to school to finish his degree. Starting in 1937, he served six terms in the House of Representatives and served in the Navy during World War II. In 1948, he was elected to the Senate. As John F. Kennedy's running mate in 1960, he was elected vice president. After Kennedy was assassinated in 1963, Johnson was sworn in as the 36th President of the United States, serving until 1969.

President Lyndon Johnson. He wanted Marshall to take the job of solicitor general. Marshall would represent the president and the nation in cases that came before the Supreme Court.

Marshall weighed the pros and cons of accepting the job. As a judge, he made $33,000 a year. Taking the solicitor general job would mean taking a pay cut. He'd only earn $28,500. He'd also lose his job security. Appeals court judges received lifetime appointments. As solicitor general, he'd only serve as long as the president was happy with the job he did. And if the president chose not to run for another term or was defeated in the next election, Marshall would likely lose his job. A new president would probably choose a new solicitor general.

But Marshall would serve as the top-ranking courtroom advocate for the entire country. He'd leave behind the daily drudgery of hearing mostly corporate cases as

an appeals court judge and be back in the battle for civil rights as those cases reached the Supreme Court. Marshall also would have direct contact with the president, the most powerful person in the country. Marshall believed that having the attention of the president could only help in his battle for equality for all Americans.

Lyndon B. Johnson chose Marshall to be the new solicitor general, making Marshall the first African-American to hold the position.

Marshall decided the pros outweighed the cons. On July 13, 1965, he accepted the job as solicitor general, becoming the first black man to ever hold the position. But Marshall and Cissy didn't want to move their family to Washington, D.C., where he would work. Instead, they decided Cissy and the boys would remain in New York. When President

Johnson heard the plan, he quickly put an end to it. He didn't want his solicitor general traveling back and forth from Washington, D.C., to New York. He wanted him nearby at all times. Johnson insisted the entire Marshall family move to the nation's capital.

The Marshalls did move to Washington, D.C., eventually settling in a mostly black neighborhood on Fourth Street in the southwest portion of the city. As their sons grew older, however, Cissy and Marshall wanted them to have more room to roam than they could find in the city. The Marshalls had

Marshall in Washington, D.C., with his family, Thurgood Jr. (left), John, and Cecilia

once been guests at the home of attorney general Ramsey Clark and his family. The Clarks lived in an all-white subdivision in the nearby suburban community of Falls Church, Virginia. Three years after the Marshalls had moved to Washington, D.C., Cissy asked the Clarks to help them find a house.

The Marshalls found a beautiful five-bedroom, three-bath home on nearby Lake Barcroft. While some people living in the area publicly expressed anger at a black family moving into the area, most welcomed them. Marshall quickly made his home a social center of the neighborhood. He often could be found barbecuing steaks, ribs, and chicken for the Clarks and other neighbors he invited to dinner.

Marshall loved his work as solicitor general. He won cases involving voting rights for blacks and other civil rights issues. He also became a trusted friend of President Johnson. Marshall was a frequent visitor at the White House. The two friends swapped stories and gossiped. Johnson also asked Marshall his opinion on issues he was facing as president.

On June 12, 1967, Marshall attended U.S. Supreme Court Justice Tom Clark's retirement party. Marshall hoped the president would name him to fill the vacancy left by Clark's retirement. After all, by then Marshall had served as solicitor general for two years. The next logical step would be to name him as the first black man to serve on the Supreme Court.

Marshall called his wife from the Oval Office to let her know about his Supreme Court nomination.

However, Johnson quickly dashed Marshall's dream. Taking Marshall aside at the party, Johnson told his solicitor general not to get his hopes up. Marshall was crushed.

But the president had not made a final decision on who should replace Clark. The next morning, Marshall was told to come to the White House. In the Oval Office, the president chatted with Marshall, who was not sure why he was there. Finally, Johnson put the uncomfortable Marshall out of his misery. "You know something, Thurgood?" Johnson asked. "I'm going to put you on the Supreme Court."

Marshall could hardly believe his ears. A little while later, Marshall and Johnson appeared in the White House Rose Garden. Johnson publicly announced his nomination of Marshall as a U.S. Supreme Court justice. Johnson said:

> *I believe it is the right thing to do, the right time to do it, the right man and the right place. I believe he has already earned his place in history, but I think it will be greatly enhanced by his service on the court.*

With prodding by the president, the Senate confirmed Marshall's nomination. Marshall took the oath of office on September 1, 1967, in the chambers of Justice Hugo Black, a former Ku Klux Klan (KKK) member from Alabama. Black and Marshall had known each other for years. Marshall had been able to overlook Black's former association with the KKK and supported Black's nomination to the Supreme Court in 1937. Black never forgot Marshall's support. As a gesture of friendship, Black volunteered his office and his services when Marshall was about to take the Supreme Court oath. Marshall became the country's 96th Supreme Court justice and the first African-American to hold the office. ❧

The Ku Klux Klan was created in the mid-1860s by Confederate Army veterans. Believing that whites are superior to other races, the group began using violence and scare tactics to keep blacks from exercising the rights they had earned after the Civil War, including the right to vote. The KKK still exists, but its numbers have dwindled. Today, it claims fewer than 6,000 members.

9 SUPREME COURT JUSTICE

❧❦❧

The Supreme Court made many landmark decisions during Marshall's tenure. Sometimes he agreed with the majority of the justices. Sometimes he didn't.

Marshall became a leader on the court in opposing the death penalty. The issue would come before the court on more than one occasion. Marshall always expressed concern that the death penalty was not fair. He pointed out that greater numbers of poor people and blacks were sentenced to death for the same crimes for which many rich whites received less serious punishments.

Marshall also stood up for the homeless, the mentally ill, and women. In 1971, the Supreme Court's schedule included two cases involving women fighting state laws restricting abortions—*Roe v. Wade* and *Doe*

Marshall was the first black man to become solicitor general and the first black Supreme Court justice.

v. Bolton. When he lived in Baltimore, Marshall had heard stories of women who suffered or died getting illegal abortions. When the other justices discussed the cases, Marshall argued that rich white women could get around the abortion laws in the United States by going to private clinics or traveling to other countries where abortion was legal. Poor women had no such choices, he said. Marshall convinced the majority of the justices, and abortion became legal in the United States.

Marshall was also a supporter of affirmative action programs. These programs gave preference to hiring minorities or admitting minorities to colleges. This was the core issue in a 1977 case filed by a white student, Allan Bakke, who was suing the University of California at Davis. Minority students with grades lower than his had been accepted to the university's medical school, but he had been turned down. The university had set aside 16 positions at the medical school for students coming from

Affirmative action programs were first ordered by President Kennedy in 1963 and then by federal agencies enforcing the Civil Rights Act of 1964 and other similar government policies. Government contractors and educational institutions, such as colleges, that received federal funds, were required to participate in affirmative action programs. They also had to meet affirmative action criteria, which included minority outreach and hiring and recruitment practices. The programs were designed to help end discrimination against women and minorities by setting aside jobs and other resources specifically for them.

disadvantaged backgrounds. Bakke, a white student, said this discriminated against him.

Marshall argued for keeping the 16 slots as they were. He urged his fellow justices to look at the university as trying to include blacks and other minorities—not trying to exclude Bakke. Years of slavery and Jim Crow laws had put blacks at a disadvantage, Marshall reminded them. They needed affirmative action programs to help them catch up. But Marshall could only convince three other justices.

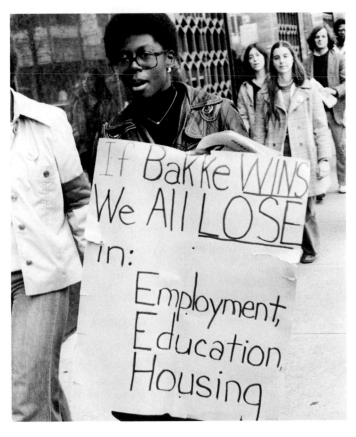

Many people protested during the Allan Bakke case against affirmative action.

Bakke won his case in a 5-4 decision.

After the Bakke decision, Marshall changed. He was growing older, and his days of drinking, smoking, and poor eating habits were taking their toll on his health. He became more grumpy and withdrawn.

Marshall did not think that the other justices understood the impact of racism. He felt this even more strongly after the ruling in the Bakke case. "What do they know about Negroes?" Marshall said of the other justices. "You can't name a member of this Court who knew anything about Negroes before he came to this Court."

Marshall was upset that the other justices did not look at affirmative action as a way of remedying past injustices suffered by blacks. He said, "There's not a white man in the country who can say, 'I never benefited by being white.'"

By the late 1970s, Marshall grew more isolated on the Supreme Court. As the more liberal justices who often sided with Marshall retired, Republican presidents appointed more conservative justices to replace them. In time, Marshall found himself voting more often against the majority instead of being a part of it as he had been in the past. He also became more publicly critical of the Court and of the presidents who came to power during his time as a justice.

His health also became an issue. For years, Marshall had suffered bouts of pneumonia. He'd even

The high court in 1982 included its first black member, Marshall (far left), and its first female member, Sandra Day O'Connor (far right.)

been hospitalized on occasion, and rumors circulated that he was near death. In October 1979, Marshall tumbled down some stairs at the Capitol and broke both his arms. Yet he bravely continued.

Marshall's eyesight began to deteriorate in the mid-1980s. He found it difficult to read. He also began to wear hearing aids in both ears. Despite his failing health, he still celebrated some big victories on the court. Among them was the 1986 case of *Batson v. Kentucky*. Marshall convinced six of his fellow justices that in criminal cases, black jurors couldn't be dismissed just because they were the same race as the defendant. Until that time, lawyers could ask that certain jurors be excluded from juries just because of their race. But although he still could win, Marshall's days on the court were numbered. ◈

10 LEGACY

❧∽❧

In June 1991, 83-year-old Thurgood Marshall announced to the other Supreme Court justices and his staff that he planned to retire. Despite Marshall's poor health, many expressed surprise at his decision. Many thought he would try to hold on until a Democratic president was in office. Democratic presidents historically have chosen more liberal candidates like Marshall for the Supreme Court. Marshall was resigning when Republican President George H.W. Bush was in office. Marshall sent the president a formal letter of resignation and wrote that he would remain in office until a replacement was confirmed by the Senate. Marshall's letter to Bush on June 27, 1991, said in part:

Thurgood Marshall brought his vision of racial equality to the Supreme Court.

The strenuous demands of court work and its related duties required or expected of a Justice appear at this time to be incompatible with my advancing age and medical condition. I, therefore, retire as an Associate Justice of the Supreme Court of the United States when my successor is qualified.

> *Clarence Thomas became the second African-American to serve on the Supreme Court. Born in 1948 in Pin Point, Georgia, Thomas earned a law degree from Yale Law School in 1974. He went on to hold several important positions, including secretary for civil rights for the U.S. Department of Education. His confirmation hearings to the Supreme Court were among the most bitter in U.S. history. Anita Hill, a former colleague, accused Thomas of harassing her when she worked for him. Despite the charges, Thomas was confirmed as a Supreme Court justice in 1991 and continues to serve on the court today.*

The process wouldn't be quick. Controversy swirled around Clarence Thomas, the man President Bush had chosen to replace Marshall. In time, however, Thomas was approved by the Senate and took Marshall's place on the court.

On the day Thurgood Marshall left the Supreme Court, he was asked what legacy he felt he left behind. "I don't know what legacy I left," he said. "It's up to the people. I guess you could say, 'He did what he could with what he had.'"

Others knew just how valuable Marshall's presence had been. He brought a perspective that had never before been seen on the

Marshall and his grandson, Thurgood William Marshall, stood together on the driveway of the Marshall family home in Falls Church, Virginia.

court. Marshall knew racism first-hand and could share his experiences. He also shared a sense of humor that could help ease some of the tensest times—even during judicial conferences when the justices argued heatedly about how the court should rule on a particular case.

One of Marshall's fellow justices, William Brennan, said:

There isn't any doubt that in a period in our history when racial issues have been among the most prominent, he brings from his own personal experience a perception of racism which is invaluable for us who have not had the same experiences. And his stories ... he's constantly breaking up the conferences, in moments of tension, with some story. ... But he can tell you from personal experience what it was like to ride for miles and miles and miles and not even be able to get a sandwich in a restaurant along the way. He couldn't get a bed to sleep in at night. And ... time after time there were not merely protests but dangerous efforts at harming him.

Once he retired, Marshall was in demand for lectures and dedications across the country, but he rarely ventured out. He did, however, serve as the guest of honor at a Fourth of July celebration at Philadelphia's Independence Mall in 1992. The 84-year-old sat in a wheelchair, but his voice was anything but weak as he talked about the continuing fight for equality for all in the United States. He said:

The battle has not yet been won; we have barely begun. Americans can do better. ... America has no choice but to do better to assure justice for all Americans, Afro and white, rich and poor, educated and illiterate. ... Our futures are bound together.

But Marshall's personal battle with his poor health was nearly finished. On January 24, 1993, at the National Naval Medical Center in Bethesda, Maryland, Thurgood Marshall died of heart failure. Marshall's body was then moved to the Great Hall of the U.S. Supreme Court in Washington, D.C., where his flag-draped coffin lay in state. Despite the cold January weather, 19,000 peopled waited in line to walk past his casket to pay their respects to Justice Marshall. Some people left roses. Someone else laid an original copy of Marshall's brief from the *Brown v. Board of Education* case on the casket.

On January 28, about 4,000 people filled the National Cathedral in Washington, D.C., for the

Marshall was only the second Supreme Court justice to have his casket placed in state at the Court's Great Hall. The first was Chief Justice Earl Warren.

funeral of Thurgood Marshall, the first black justice of the Supreme Court. Chief Justice of the United States William Rehnquist spoke. He reminded everyone of the words above the entrance to the Supreme Court—Equal Justice Under Law—and then said, "Surely no one individual did more to make these words a reality than Thurgood Marshall."

Marshall's body was buried in a private ceremony at Arlington National Cemetery in Arlington, Virginia.

Tributes to Marshall could be seen on television and in newspapers. An editorial in *The Washington Afro American* newspaper discussed his place in history among some of the more famous black leaders:

> *We make movies about Malcolm X, we get a holiday to honor Dr. Martin Luther King, but every day we live with the legacy of Justice Thurgood Marshall.*

Benjamin Hooks, executive director of the NAACP, agreed. "It's my belief that without Thurgood Marshall, we would still be riding in the back of the bus, going to separate schools and drinking 'colored' water," he said, referring to the separate water fountains black people were once forced to use in the days of Jim Crow laws.

Others pointed out that Marshall's heart was in all the decisions he made. "Not all great men are good

Marshall is buried at Arlington National Cemetery in Arlington, Virginia.

men," one reporter said. "Marshall was both."

Thanks to Marshall's hard work and courage, many people of all races are free today to live in any neighborhood they choose, attend any school they wish, and be treated equally in the workplace. He also broke racial boundaries in the justice system. He opened the door for people of all races to serve on juries, to become judges, and to even be named to the highest court in the nation—the U.S. Supreme Court. 🍂

MARSHALL'S LIFE

1908
Born July 2 in
Baltimore, Maryland

1914
Family moves
back to Baltimore
from Harlem

1921
Named captain of his
high school debate
team as a freshman

1920

1919
The Treaty
of Versailles
officially ends
World War I

1920
American women
get the right to vote

League of Women Voters

1909
The National
Association for
the Advancement
of Colored People
(NAACP) is founded

WORLD EVENTS

1925

Graduates from high school and starts classes at Lincoln University

1929

Marries Vivian Burey on September 4

1930

Graduates from Lincoln University in January

1930

1928

Penicillin, the first antibiotic, is discovered by Scottish scientist Alexander Fleming

1930

Designs for the first jet engine are submitted to the Patent Office in Britain

MARSHALL'S LIFE

1936
Moves to New York to take full-time job with the NAACP

1938
Charles Hamilton Houston leaves NAACP; Marshall is put in charge of all court cases

1933
Graduates from Howard University School of Law and opens his law firm in Baltimore

1935

1933
Nazi leader Adolf Hitler is named chancellor of Germany

1936
African-American athlete Jesse Owens wins four gold medals at the Olympic Games in Berlin in the face of Nazi racial discrimination

WORLD EVENTS

1954

Argues *Brown v. Board of Education* before the U.S. Supreme Court

1955

Wife Vivian dies February 11; marries Cecilia Suyat December 17

1946

Awarded the Spingarn Medal by the NAACP

1960

1953

Sir Edmund Hillary of New Zealand and Tenzing Norgay of Nepal are the first two men to reach the summit of Mount Everest

1946

Nazi war criminals are executed after trials in Nuremberg, Germany

1955

Disneyland opens in southern California

MARSHALL'S LIFE

1961

Appointed judge
of the U.S. Second
Circuit Court of
Appeals

1965

Becomes solicitor
general of the
United States

1967

Nominated and
confirmed as
justice of the U.S.
Supreme Court

1965

1961

A fortified wall
is built in Berlin,
dividing East and
West Germany

1965

Soviet cosmonaut
Alexei Leonov
becomes the first
person to walk
in space

1967

The first heart
transplant is
performed by Dr.
Christiaan Barnard in
South Africa; the
surgery is a success
but the patient lives
only 18 days

WORLD EVENTS

1977

Argues Allan Bakke case for affirmative action

1991

Announced retirement from the Supreme Court

1993

Dies January 24 in Bethesda, Maryland

1995

1989

The Berlin Wall is torn down, marking the end of the Cold War

1991

The Soviet Union collapses and is replaced by the Commonwealth of Independent States

1994

Genocide of 500,000 to 1 million of the minority Tutsi group by rival Hutu people in Rwanda

DATE OF BIRTH: July 2, 1908

BIRTHPLACE: Baltimore, Maryland

FATHER: William "Willie" Marshall

MOTHER: Norma Marshall

EDUCATION: Graduated from Lincoln
University in 1930 and
Howard University
School of Law in 1933

FIRST SPOUSE: Vivian Burey (1911–1955)

DATE OF MARRIAGE: September 4, 1929

SECOND SPOUSE: Cecilia Suyat (1927–)

DATE OF MARRIAGE: December 17, 1955

CHILDREN: Thurgood Marshall Jr.
(1956–)
John W. Marshall (1958–)

DATE OF DEATH: January 24, 1993

PLACE OF BURIAL: Arlington National
Cemetery, Arlington,
Virginia

FURTHER READING

Aldred, Lisa. *Thurgood Marshall: Supreme Court Justice*. Philadelphia: Chelsea House Publishers, 2005.

Conaway, Judith. *Brown v. Board of Education*. Minneapolis: Compass Point Books, 2007.

Lindop, Edmund. *The Changing Supreme Court*. New York: Franklin Watts, 1995.

McIntire, Suzanne. *The American Heritage Book of Great American Speeches for Young People*. New York: Wiley, 2001.

LOOK FOR MORE SIGNATURE LIVES
BOOKS ABOUT THIS ERA:

Clara Barton: *Founder of the American Red Cross.*

George Washington Carver: *Scientist, Inventor, and Teacher*

Amelia Earhart: *Legendary Aviator*

Thomas Alva Edison: *Great American Inventor*

Yo-Yo Ma: *Renowned Concert Cellist*

Annie Oakley: *American Sharpshooter*

Will Rogers: *Cowboy, Comedian, and Commentator*

Amy Tan: *Writer and Storyteller*

Madam C.J. Walker: *Entrepreneur and Millionaire*

Booker T. Washington: *Innovative Educator*

ON THE WEB

For more information on *Thurgood Marshall,* use FactHound.

1. Go to *www.facthound.com*
2. Type in this book ID: 0756518776
3. Click on the *Fetch It* button.

FactHound will find the best Web sites for you.

HISTORIC SITES

U.S. Supreme Court
1 First St. N.E.
Washington, DC 20543
202/479-3000
The Supreme Court of the United States, the highest judicial branch in the nation

Brown v. Board of Education National Historic Site
1515 S.E. Monroe St.
Topeka, KS 66612
785/354-4273
Site located at Monroe Elementary School, one of four segregated elementary schools in Topeka, Kansas, which was the target of the landmark decision *Brown v. Board of Education*

abortion
the ending of a pregnancy

integration
opening up a place or organization to all, regardless of race

loophole
a way to bypass a law

lynched
killed by a mob without a trial, usually by hanging

manslaughter
the unlawful killing of a person without meaning to do so

oppression
an unjust or cruel exercise of authority or power

psychologist
person who studies people's minds, emotions, and the ways they behave

reprimanded
sharply scolded

segregation
the practice of separating people of different races

sharecroppers
farmers who work the land in exchange for housing, food, and part of the profits

stereotypes
overly simplified ideas and prejudiced attitudes about a group of people

supplement
an addition to something

tuition
money paid to attend a school

Chapter 1

Page 10, line 10: Juan Williams. *Thurgood Marshall: American Revolutionary*, New York: Times Books, 1998, p. 226.

Page 11, line 4: Ibid., p. 227.

Page 13, line 4: Howard Ball. *A Defiant Life: Thurgood Marshall & the Persistence of Racism in America.* New York: Crown Publishers, Inc., 1998, p. 41.

Chapter 3

Page 25, line 14: *Thurgood Marshall: American Revolutionary*, p. 35.

Page 25, line 23: Michael D. Davis and Hunter R. Clark. *Thurgood Marshall: Warrior at the Bar, Rebel on the Bench.* New York: Carol Publishing Group, 1992, p. 37.

Page 26, line 4: *Thurgood Marshall: American Revolutionary*, pp. 35–36.

Chapter 4

Page 36, line 1: Ibid., p. 56.

Page 37, line 13: Ibid., p. 59.

Page 39, line 1: Ibid.

Page 39, line 12: Ibid., p. 60.

Chapter 5

Page 44, line 21: Ibid., p. 68.

Page 46, line 5: Ibid., p. 70.

Page 47, line 13: *A Defiant Life: Thurgood Marshall & the Persistence of Racism in America*, p. 49.

Chapter 6

Page 52, line 11: *Thurgood Marshall: Warrior at the Bar, Rebel on the Bench*, p. 108.

Page 56, line 15: *Thurgood Marshall: American Revolutionary*, p. 141.

Chapter 7

Page 63, line 13: Ibid., p. 201.

Page 69, line 7: Ibid., p. 229.

Page 69, line 15: *A Defiant Life: Thurgood Marshall & the Persistence of Racism in America*, p. 139.

Page 73, line 1: *Thurgood Marshall: American Revolutionary*, p. 287.

Chapter 8

Page 80, line 10: Ibid., p. 11.

Page 81, line 3: *Thurgood Marshall: Warrior at the Bar, Rebel on the Bench*, p. 13.

Chapter 9

Page 86, line 9: *A Defiant Life: Thurgood Marshall & the Persistence of Racism in America*, p. 205.

Page 86, line 15: Ibid.

Chapter 10

Page 90, line 1: Carl T. Rowan. *Dream Makers, Dream Breakers: The World of Justice Thurgood Marshall*. Boston: Little, Brown and Company, 1993, p. 403.

Page 90, line 22: *Thurgood Marshall: Warrior at the Bar, Rebel at the Bench*, p. 382.

Page 92, line 1: *Dream Makers, Dream Breakers: The World of Justice Thurgood Marshall*, p. 416.

Page 92, line 25: *Thurgood Marshall: Warrior at the Bar, Rebel at the Bench*, p. 369.

Page 94, line 6: "Raising the Bar: Pioneers in the Legal Profession." American Bar Association. 19 May 2006. http://abanet.org/publiced/tm.html

Page 94, line 15: *Thurgood Marshall: American Revolutionary*, p. xv.

Page 94, line 20: *A Defiant Life: Thurgood Marshall & the Persistence of Racism in America*, p. 388.

Page 94, line 27: Ibid.

Ball, Howard. *A Defiant Life: Thurgood Marshall & the Persistence of Racism in America.* New York: Crown Publishers, Inc., 1998.

Davis, Michael D., and Hunter R. Clark. *Thurgood Marshall: Warrior at the Bar, Rebel on the Bench.* New York: Carol Publishing Group, 1992.

Rowan, Carl T. *Dream Makers, Dream Breakers: The World of Justice Thurgood Marshall.* Boston: Little, Brown and Company, 1993.

Williams, Juan. *Thurgood Marshall: American Revolutionary.* New York: Times Books, 1998.

Brenda Haugen started in the newspaper business and had a career as an award-winning journalist before finding her niche as an author. Since then, she has written and edited many books, most of them for children. A graduate of the University of North Dakota in Grand Forks, Brenda lives in North Dakota with her family.

Image Credits